THE COOK

by

Eduardo Machado

SAMUEL
FRENCH

FOUNDED 1830

New York Hollywood London Toronto

WWW.SAMUELFRENCH.COM

IMPORTANT BILLING AND CREDIT REQUIREMENTS

All producers of *THE COOK* *must* give credit to the Author of the Play in all programs distributed in connection with performances of the Play, and in all instances in which the title of the Play appears for the purposes of advertising, publicizing or otherwise exploiting the Play and /or a production. The name of the Author must appear on a separate line on which no other name appears, immediately following the title and must appear in size of type not less than fifty percent of the size of the title type.

In addition, the following credit *must* appear in all programs distributed in connection with the Work:

THE COOK
originally produced
December 2003 - January 2004
by INTAR, New York

THE COOK by Eduardo Machado had its New York premiere at INTAR Hispanic American Arts Center, Max Ferrá Founder and Producing Artistic Director, running November 11, 2003 to January 18, 2004. The production was directed by Michael John Garcés with the following cast:

ZABRYNA GUEVARA..........................Gladys
JASON MADERA....................................Carlos
MAGGIE BOFILL.....................Adria/Lourdes
NILAJA SUN..................................Elena/Rosa
JASON QUARLES................................Julio

PLACE: A mansion in El Vedado,a district of La Habana, Cuba.

Act I - TIME: 1958

Act II - TIME: 1972

Act III - TIME: 1997

ACT I

(A mansion in El Vedado, a district of La Habana, Cuba. December 31st, 1958. Gladys, the cook, is talking to her husband Carlos, the chauffeur. They are both in their early thirties. They are in the kitchen. The kitchen is luxurious. They are in the middle of serving a New Year's Eve party. There is a big bucket of homemade ice cream on top of a counter. Carlos is trying to steal a taste with a spoon. Gladys is brushing his hand away)

GLADYS. No, Carlos!

CARLOS. Just a little bit, baby. Just a little taste of something sweet on my lips.

GLADYS. Kiss me then.

CARLOS. Come on.

GLADYS. My lips are sweeter than any dessert.

CARLOS. Baby! A taste, that's all.

GLADYS. It's for the party.

CARLOS. They won't know.

GLADYS. But I will.

CARLOS. They're all drunk. Who cares.

GLADYS. I care.

CARLOS. Come on, one taste.

GLADYS. I said no.

CARLOS. Oh, really.

GLADYS. Yes.

CARLOS. Are you going to tell me what to do?

GLADYS. That's right.

CARLOS. It's New Year's Eve. Something's gotta be for me.

GLADYS. I don't mix business with pleasure.

CARLOS. They won't mind.

GLADYS. But I mind. It's my job. What if we run out?

THE COOK

CARLOS. Are you kidding?

GLADYS. We work for them.

CARLOS. So?

GLADYS. So we don't eat their food. Unless they tell us to.

CARLOS. I'm having some and that's that.

(He takes a little spoonful.)

GLADYS. You'll never learn.

CARLOS. This is good! This is god dammed delicious!

GLADYS. Really?

CARLOS. Baby.

GLADYS. I am your baby.

CARLOS. What a cook!

GLADYS.Well.

CARLOS. What fruit did you put in it?

GLADYS. Guess.

CARLOS. I gotta take another bite.

GLADYS. Nothing like home made ice cream.

CARLOS. Another taste, please.

GLADYS. Use another spoon.

CARLOS. Why?

GLADYS. That one has your saliva on it.

CARLOS. Jesus!

(She gives him another spoon.)

GLADYS. Don't complain, you're getting another bite.

(CARLOS takes the other spoon.)

GLADYS. Taste it.

(He does.)

    CARLOS. Mango?
    GLADYS. No.
    CARLOS. Papaya?
    GLADYS. Way off.
    CARLOS. Guayaba, has to be guayaba.
    GLADYS. Guayaba? For the Señora Adria Santana? Are you kidding?
    CARLOS. How do I know?
    GLADYS. She has a more delicate palate.
    CARLOS. Really? Well... Well...
    GLADYS. It's strawberry.
    CARLOS. Hmm. Strawberry.
    GLADYS. Do you like it better than the lime?
    CARLOS. Better than the lime?
    GLADYS. Yes, do you? You had the lime last year. Bring in Fifty-Eight with lime, Fifty-Nine with strawberry.
    CARLOS. And Sixty with rum?
    GLADYS. I don't know about the future.
    CARLOS. I do.
    GLADYS. I don't want to hear about it.
    CARLOS. You're gonna have to...

(ELENA ENTERS.)

    ELENA. Its fun!
    GLADYS. Elena.
    GLADYS. You're so sweet.

(ELENA EXITS.)

    CARLOS. Give me another spoonful.

(GLADYS laughs.)

GLADYS. When it's finished.

CARLOS. It's delicious. It has to be finished.

GLADYS. No! Now it's going to turn into "Baked Alaska"!

CARLOS. What?

GLADYS. Cake underneath, meringue on top. Then right before the New Year, I put it in the oven to brown.

CARLOS. Are you crazy?

GLADYS. No.

CARLOS. It will melt!

GLADYS. Apparently not.

CARLOS. Impossible.

GLADYS. Señora Adria had it in New York.

CARLOS. Another American invention.

GLADYS. Yes, apparently their ice cream does not melt. And their shit does not stink, and they don't overthrow their leaders with revolutions.

CARLOS. See? You talked about it.

GLADYS. You tricked me.

CARLOS. You know what's going on.

GLADYS. Maybe.

CARLOS. I'm sure of it. We're going to get rid of all the fucking foreigners that are trying to control our country. When I was at the Union Hall, they said it was only days away... that Batista's army was going to turn around and....

GLADYS. I don't want to know.

(We hear a bell ring.)

GLADYS. They need more hors d'oeuvres. Go.

CARLOS. I'm the chauffeur, not a waiter.

THE COOK

GLADYS. It's a big party.

(The bell rings again.)

GLADYS. Pick up the tray and stop bullshitting.

CARLOS. Didn't you hire two of your cousins?

GLADYS. They needed the work.

CARLOS. Why can't they take the trays of hors d' oeuvres?

GLADYS. They're out there working. You are the one that is in here eating.

CARLOS. If someone wants me to drive them somewhere, I will.

GLADYS. It's the first time they're trying to serve at a big classy party. Please I need you to help them...

CARLOS. Serve?

GLADYS. Yes!

CARLOS. Obviously your cousins are just a bunch of...

GLADYS. Go. Help them. Before you say my cousins are lazy niggers!

CARLOS. Well...

GLADYS. Oh, you're so white!

CARLOS. Whiter than Batista.

GLADYS. Not to them.

CARLOS. And you're what? A drop of espresso in a cup full of milk?

GLADYS. I know who I am.

CARLOS. Really?

GLADYS. Absolutely.

CARLOS. A lady in waiting. To the great Adria. Pure white milk, descended from Spain. Adria Santana.

GLADYS. No. I'm not a lady in waiting.

CARLOS. I'm surprised you don't want the title.

GLADYS. I'm a great cook.

CARLOS. So?

THE COOK

GLADYS. That's who I am. Take the tray and work.

(She hands him the tray. CARLOS admires the hors d'oeuvres.)

CARLOS. Beautiful.

GLADYS. See? I can cook.

CARLOS. You should be working at a fancy hotel.

GLADYS. At hotels, cooks are men.

CARLOS. Come the revolution...

GLADYS. Cooks at hotels will still be men.

CARLOS. You're wrong.

GLADYS. I like it here. I like where I am.

CARLOS. Funny I thought you were waiting for the revolution, just like I am.

GLADYS. Well, I am not..

CARLOS. Why not?

GLADYS. They don't like it.

CARLOS. Your masters?

GLADYS. The people we work for.

CARLOS. Well, the people you work for have helped turn our country into a floating Casino. They have made us dependent on the U.S. dollars and the U.S. tourists — and all they want is a little bit of pussy and a place where they can gamble, drink and piss. Piss all over us.

GLADYS. Shut up!

CARLOS. Fidel Castro's revolution will give power and dignity back to the people of Cuba.

GLADYS. Jesus, Carlos, the ballroom is filled with Batista's people.

CARLOS. Second-tier Batista people.

GLADYS. Second-tier for sure. But still powerful enough to have you killed.

CARLOS. Fidel Castro's revolution. Repeat it. Revolution. Fidel Castro. Come on, get used to it. Revolution.

GLADYS. Stop it!

THE COOK

(The bell rings again.)

    CARLOS. They're not patient either.
    GLADYS. Please!
    CARLOS. What, sweetie?
    GLADYS. Serve them.
    CARLOS. Meat pies, my favorites.
    GLADYS. They're stuffed with crab.
    CARLOS. Something else from the USA?
    GLADYS. No. My recipe. Cuban.

(CARLOS picks up one of the crab pies.)

    CARLOS. Then I want to swallow it whole.

(He swallows the puff pastry.)

    CARLOS. Tastes like you.

(The bell rings.)

    GLADYS. Yes?
    CARLOS. Salty, yet sweet.
    GLADYS. Cuban, like I said.
    CARLOS. Yes.

(He starts to kiss her.)

    GLADYS. Honey, please, go.

(CARLOS leaves. GLADYS looks through a cookbook.)

THE COOK

GLADYS. *(Reading.)* "Preheat the oven to 450 degrees."

(She goes and lights the oven. She reads the cookbook.)

GLADYS. *(Reading.)* "Cut the cake into one-inch squares. Put the squares on a cookie tray. Place the ice cream on top, but make sure it's hard." *(To herself.)* It's so hard I can't scoop it out yet. *(Reading.)* "Cover it with meringue. Then put it in the oven till the meringue is golden. Serve it immediately." *(Adria enters.)* This is not going to be easy. Baked Alaska for fifty, maybe sixty?

(ADRIA has walked in during the last speech. She is in her late thirties, elegant. She is wearing an evening gown, and noticeable, rubies in her ears and around her neck.)

ADRIA. Who knows?

GLADYS. I'll send a cousin to count the guests. All right, next, whip the meringue and make it firm, like "The Snows of Kilimanjaro."

ADRIA. So you did read the book I gave you.

GLADYS. Yes I love Hemingway. What a mind!

ADRIA. Yes. He's a drunk, you know. You can always see him drinking in every bar in town. But he's a great writer. Maybe he's a tortured soul. Maybe that's why he drinks. Maybe that's why he writes. Who knows? One day, the booze will destroy his brain and the rest of him, so he won't be able to write anymore.

GLADYS. I hope not. I love his stories.

ADRIA. Why?

GLADYS. He loves us. He loves La Habana.

ADRIA. Yes, well, what's here not to love?

GLADYS. Nothing.

ADRIA. What time is it now?

GLADYS. Twenty-five to twelve.

THE COOK

(Pause.)

ADRIA. You like the new cookbook by Nitza Villapol?

GLADYS. It's as good as her television show.

ADRIA. I'm sure you're a much better cook.

GLADYS. Señora! How could that be?

ADRIA. You're really good.

GLADYS. But Nitza's on television. Women all over this country watch her.

ADRIA. Yes?

GLADYS. And worship her.

ADRIA. So?

GLADYS. So?

ADRIA. You're better.

GLADYS. Well, thank you.

ADRIA. We should send you to Paris, to a French cooking school, then you'd show them how gifted you really are.

GLADYS. I'm not.

ADRIA. Believe me. I know.

GLADYS. Really?

ADRIA. I've been to Paris.

GLADYS. I remember.

ADRIA. I had a meal in the most expensive restaurant in Paris. And I told my mother, "Gladys is better."

GLADYS. She agreed?

ADRIA. She said, "Imagine if she knew these recipes. There would be no stopping her. You'd lose her."

GLADYS. Never.

ADRIA. I'm a very lucky woman to have someone like you cooking for me.

GLADYS. All right. Flatter me. It's the holidays.

ADRIA. No, not flattery. Facts. Put the ice cream away, or it'll get too soft.

THE COOK

GLADYS. But I need to be able to scoop it out. It's like a rock now.

ADRIA. We have plenty of time.

GLADYS. But...

ADRIA. Everything is going to happen a little bit later.

GLADYS. What do you mean?

ADRIA. We need to play with time.

GLADYS. New Year's is at midnight no matter what.

ADRIA. Not this year! Ask Carlos to set the clocks back an hour. Mr. Santana is not here yet, and I cannot greet the New Year without him.

GLADYS. But...

ADRIA. Those bitches out there would start saying that he has a mistress — and he doesn't have a mistress.

GLADYS. Of course not.

ADRIA. Maybe their husbands need something somewhere else.

GLADYS. Maybe.

ADRIA. I mean, look at them, so tight...

GLADYS. Yes.

ADRIA. Or overly voluptuous.

GLADYS. Fat.

ADRIA. They don't walk enough.

GLADYS. You think?

ADRIA. They don't fuck enough.

GLADYS. You're sure?

ADRIA. Too many bonbons instead of cocks.

GLADYS. Religious girls.

ADRIA. The worst kind.

GLADYS. Yes.

ADRIA. That's for damn sure.

GLADYS. Jesus, forgive us.

ADRIA. There's enough woman in me for twenty men. My husband, he knows it. He worships me. My skin, my eyes, my breasts, my hips, my ass.

THE COOK

GLADYS. You are beautiful.

ADRIA. So are you.

GLADYS. Thank you.

ADRIA. I mean it.

GLADYS. I appreciate it.

ADRIA. If it wasn't for the fact that you work for me, we could be friends.

GLADYS. I feel we are.

ADRIA. My mother thinks it's cruel to be friends with people that work for you.

(Pause.)

GLADYS. We're a certain kind of friends.

ADRIA. What kind?

GLADYS. Someone who's always there, next to you. nothing has to be said.

ADRIA. Yes.

GLADYS. Nothing has to be said.

ADRIA. But I want to.

GLADYS. Fine.

ADRIA. I have a great affection towards you.

GLADYS. The feeling is mutual, Señora.

(They embrace.)

ADRIA. Oh.

GLADYS. Señora.

(ADRIA lets out a scream.)

ADRIA. Ay! Ay!

GLADYS. What's wrong? Señora.

ADRIA. Sometimes when a victim is being strangled, she lets out a scream.

GLADYS. Tell me who's strangling you.

ADRIA. Fidel Castro!

(Pause.)

GLADYS. Oh.

ADRIA. You understand?

GLADYS. I'm trying.

ADRIA. The bastard.

GLADYS. Things look bad?

ADRIA. Maybe.

GLADYS. You can trust me.

(ADRIA looks at Gladys.)

ADRIA. I can, can't I?

GLADYS. Yes.

ADRIA. No matter what.

GLADYS. Yes.

ADRIA. I want to. I want to tell you.

GLADYS. I want to hear it.

(ADRIA starts to cry.)

GLADYS. You're crying.

ADRIA. Yes, things are bad. Disaster.

GLADYS. I could feel it.

ADRIA. And the tragedy is I could be happy if it wasn't for that bastard and his god dammed revolution. Gladys, I'm pregnant!

GLADYS. Finally!

ADRIA. Just when I thought it was all going to go away.

THE COOK

GLADYS. I knew it would happen.

ADRIA. I'll be able to lie about my age.

GLADYS. Yes!

ADRIA. With a baby in my arms, they'll believe I'm just thirty.

GLADYS. Good.

ADRIA. Yes. But the father does nothing but worry. Worry about his future. His money. His life.

GLADYS. The baby didn't make him happy? He's been waiting for twelve years.

ADRIA. I haven't told him.

GLADYS. Oh.

ADRIA. I wanted to be sure.

GLADYS. Of course.

ADRIA. But I'm going to tell him tonight.

GLADYS. The situation will change.

ADRIA. Yes.

GLADYS. Feel better.

ADRIA. I do.

GLADYS. Good.

ADRIA. Yes, let's start with your watch.

GLADYS. Why not?

(GLADYS gives Adria her watch.)

ADRIA. Nice.

GLADYS. You know Carlos.

ADRIA. It reads 11:40, but... Puff! Magic... and it's 10:40. And now, mine. Your husband can do the rest.

(JULIO ENTERS.)

JULIO. Seventy-two guests.

THE COOK

(JULIO EXITS.)

ADRIA. Do we have enough hors d'oeuvres?
GLADYS. Of course.
ADRIA. What a silly question.
GLADYS. You know me.
ADRIA. Always making double than what's needed.
GLADYS. My crime.
ADRIA. Yes, we'll keep feeding them. Keep those hypocritical sons of bitches happy.

(CARLOS ENTERS.)

ADRIA. Carlos, please, my husband is going to be late.
CARLOS. Yes?
ADRIA. So New Year's is going to have to be later.
CARLOS. How?
GLADYS. Set the clocks back an hour.
CARLOS. What?
GLADYS. That's right.
ADRIA. Yes. Set the clocks back an hour. Ours are.

(She shows him her watch.)

ADRIA. It's an hour earlier.
CARLOS. But.
ADRIA. By my watch, in my house.
CARLOS. But....
ADRIA. It's what I've decided.
CARLOS. Who's going to believe...?
GLADYS. It's what she needs you to do.
CARLOS. And you agree with her?
GLADYS. Yes.

THE COOK

CARLOS. But...

ADRIA. That's what I want at my party.

GLADYS. That's what she wants.

CARLOS. Fine.

ADRIA. Do it in a way that they don't notice.

CARLOS. Sure!

ADRIA. Good.

GLADYS. Settled.

ADRIA. Yes.

GLADYS. Easy.

ADRIA. It is.

GLADYS. So, stop worrying.

CARLOS. How about their watches?

ADRIA. We didn't think of that.

GLADYS. They'll think they're fast.

ADRIA. Yes. Right.

CARLOS. Whatever you say.

ADRIA. Start with the big one in the hallway. Gladys, the ice cream — in the freezer!

GLADYS. It's in there already.

ADRIA. Good.

(ADRIA leaves.)

GLADYS. Go change the clocks.

CARLOS. Sometimes I look at all this and wonder why it's not mine.

GLADYS. Fate.

CARLOS. Or the color of my skin.

GLADYS. So now you're black.

CARLOS. To them. Or maybe it's that I was born poor.

GLADYS. Jesus loves the poor more than the rich.

CARLOS. Really?

GLADYS. Don't get bitter. Go and change the clocks.

THE COOK

CARLOS. Playing with time.

GLADYS. Yes. We are. She said if I didn't work for her we could be friends.

CARLOS. And that made you feel good.

GLADYS. Yes, warm.

CARLOS. I want more.

GLADYS. That could be dangerous.

CARLOS. Don't worry about me. I'm gonna win.

GLADYS. That would be nice.

CARLOS. And I'll buy you a restaurant.

GLADYS. What for? You're going to get rid of the tourists.

CARLOS. Cubans will still eat out.

GLADYS. Dreamer.

CARLOS. But that's what you love about me.

GLADYS. That's what I love and what scares me.

(She kisses him.)

CARLOS. Nice. So do I really have to change the clocks?

GLADYS. If you want another kiss. Go. She's gonna ring the bell if you don't do it soon..

(The bell rings.)

GLADYS. See? Send in one of my cousins. I need help. I have to make more hors d'oeuvres.

CARLOS. So you don't have it all under control.

GLADYS. I will.

(CARLOS EXITS.)

GLADYS. Time changes. Time is always moving. The cookbook is always the same. But if you improvise on the recipe in the slightest way,

THE COOK

it changes, it becomes a whole new dish.

(She grabs her cookbook and sits in a chair.)

GLADYS. "To cook in a minute." Nitza, help me. Save me. I need your minute. Right now, today, when a minute is everything. Should I look under breads and muffins? Or sandwiches and petit sandwiches? Petit sandwiches, on page 301. Stuffed eggs? No, that's for a day on the beach, not New Year's.

(JULIO, Gladys' cousin, walks in. He is very dark, lean and beautiful. He is twenty.)

JULIO. You need me?
GLADYS. What?
JULIO. Carlos said you needed me.
GLADYS. He did?
JULIO. Yes.
GLADYS. I do.
JULIO. Well, here I am.
GLADYS. I'm going to make finger sandwiches.
JULIO. What kind?
GLADYS. I haven't decided yet.
JULIO. Oh. I think...
GLADYS. Take off the crust.
JULIO. I know how.
GLADYS. Good.
JULIO. I like being with you in the kitchen.
GLADYS. In the drawer. The bread knife.
JULIO. Sure.
GLADYS. The drawer on the left.
JULIO. I'm opening it.
GLADYS. You know what it looks like?

THE COOK

JULIO. What?
GLADYS. The knife.
JULIO. Well, I think...
GLADYS. Very long and very flat.
JULIO. That's right. Very long and very flat.

(JULIO opens the drawer.)

GLADYS. I've decided!
JULIO. What's it going to be?
GLADYS. I'll make a spread with cream cheese and pimento and another one with anchovies.

(JULIO starts to slice the bread. GLADYS starts getting cream cheese and the other ingredients and starts making the spread. GLADYS starts humming a song. JULIO starts doing some dance steps.)

GLADYS. Dancing while you work.
JULIO. As long as you get the work done.
GLADYS. True.

(GLADYS hums along and does a couple of steps.)

GLADYS. How long has it been since I've gone to a dance on New Year's?
JULIO. Pity.
GLADYS. That's what happens when you work for a living.
JULIO. Are you running out of food?
GLADYS. We might.
JULIO. It's almost midnight.
GLADYS. At this house New Year's is going to take longer than you think.
JULIO. Oh.

THE COOK

GLADYS. High society. Or is it odd society?

JULIO. I like it. The men in their white tuxedos. They look beautiful, don't you think?

GLADYS. This is a classy crowd.

JULIO. La Habana is one of the few places where you can wear white at New Year's.

GLADYS. But not the women.

JULIO. In the rest of the world it's black.

GLADYS. You like fashion?

JULIO. Yes.

GLADYS. I see.

JULIO. So?

GLADYS. Nothing.

JULIO. Good. Nothing wrong with liking fashion.

GLADYS. Nothing.

JULIO. I'm glad you feel that way.

GLADYS. I'm not backwards.

JULIO. I know.

GLADYS. Good.

JULIO. I might want to be a hairdresser.

GLADYS. You mean a barber?

JULIO. No, when it's for women, it's called a hairdresser or a coiffeur.

GLADYS. Want to be near the ladies, huh? You are a sly one.

JULIO. For sure!

GLADYS. How's your girlfriend?

JULIO. She left me.

GLADYS. I'm sorry.

JULIO. I'm young.

GLADYS. Are you heart broken?

JULIO. We had a split, that's all.

GLADYS. Well.

JULIO. Your bread is sliced.

GLADYS. The spread is ready. Here we go!

THE COOK

JULIO. You want me to help you spread it?
GLADYS. Men are not good at doing things like this.
JULIO. Maybe.
GLADYS. Not really.

(GLADYS spreads the paste.)

JULIO. You want me to make the anchovy spread?
GLADYS. I'm the cook.
JULIO. In great restaurants, cooks are men.
GLADYS. Not in this one!
JULIO. Of course not.

(JULIO looks at his watch.)

GLADYS. Beautiful, huh?

(GLADYS arranges sandwiches in a tray. Julio looks at his watch.)

JULIO. Fifteen minutes till 1959.
GLADYS. An hour and fifteen minutes!
JULIO. No. My watch is right. It runs perfectly.
GLADYS. This house is on a different time.
JULIO. What?
GLADYS. We set all the clocks back an hour.

(The bell rings.)

GLADYS. Oh God! She needs the hors d'oeuvres!

(GLADYS starts to cry.)

JULIO. Don't cry.

THE COOK

GLADYS. Tonight, I think tonight the world is going to turn inside out!

JULIO. I see.

GLADYS. Do you?

JULIO. I listen to the news.

GLADYS. We all do.

JULIO. We all hear everything and then pretend we didn't hear it.

GLADYS. It's only human.

JULIO. Yes.

(Pause.)

GLADYS. I gotta work.

JULIO. Please let me help you.

GLADYS. There is no other choice.

JULIO. I'll do a good job. I promise.

GLADYS. I know you will, Julio.

(The bell rings. ELENA ENTERS.)

ELENA. This is hard!

GLADYS. Chop the anchovies real fine.

JULIO. Done!

GLADYS. I'll arrange another tray.

(She starts to work. The phone rings. She answers it, but continues to work.)

GLADYS. Santana's... Oh señor... Yes, we are waiting for you. She's in the party. I'm in the kitchen. New Year's is waiting for you... How? We set the clocks back... *(She laughs)* Yes, her idea of course... An hour... Believe me, it's not going to happen till you get here... We do have our ways... Oh, Señora Adria... Yes! Yes, Señora... Excuse me.

THE COOK

(CARLOS walks in with an empty tray.)

CARLOS. No one is falling for the time change.

GLADYS. We got to keep them eating.

JULIO. "Let them eat cake!"

GLADYS. Not yet.

JULIO. No, that's what Marie Antoinette said.

CARLOS. Who?

JULIO. She was the Queen of France when the revolutionaries were at the door.

GLADYS. There are no revolutionaries at the door.

(GLADYS starts to work.)

CARLOS. How do you know this stuff?

JULIO. I go to the movies.

CARLOS. Too much of the time, if you ask me.

JULIO. I didn't ask you.

GLADYS. Carlos, fill the tray with those sandwiches. Julio, spread more paste on another loaf. I'll cut them. I have to make sure they look right on the tray. The way something looks is everything!

CARLOS. Nothing like a woman's touch.

GLADYS. Really?

CARLOS. Really.

GLADYS. Thank you.

CARLOS. I know you're nervous, but remember that I love you.

GLADYS. No matter what changes?

CARLOS. Change is good.

GLADYS. Go serve the sandwiches, please.

(CARLOS eats one.)

THE COOK

CARLOS. Delicious.
GLADYS. Don't eat anymore!
CARLOS. I'm your taster.
GLADYS. Go.
CARLOS. I will, this time without a fight.

(CARLOS goes.)

JULIO. I'm going to make more.
GLADYS. Good.
JULIO. I did a good job with the last ones.
GLADYS. Yes you did, Julio. A very good job. I'll get another tray.
JULIO. They sure can eat, the ruling class.
GLADYS. So can the working class.
JULIO. Yeah.

(GLADYS gets a tray and puts doilies on it.)

JULIO. Chic.
GLADYS. Yes, aren't they?
JULIO. For sure.
GLADYS. Not too old fashioned?
JULIO. No.

(They start setting sandwiches on the tray.)

JULIO. How long have you been working here?
GLADYS. In this house?
JULIO. Yes.
GLADYS. Twelve years.
JULIO. Long time.
GLADYS. Maybe.
JULIO. Seems like a long time to me.

THE COOK

GLADYS. I came over to this house when Adria got married. I started working for her family when I was thirteen. I started doing the laundry, ironing simple things. Then I showed a talent for cooking and Señora Santana's mother encouraged it. She is responsible for my vocation.

JULIO. And you're grateful.

GLADYS. Grateful? No.

JULIO. All right.

GLADYS. Indebted.

(ADRIA is there. She is wearing a black mink coat and is carrying a beach bag.)

JULIO. My God! What a vision!

ADRIA. What's your name?

JULIO. Julio Gómez.

GLADYS. He's my cousin.

JULIO. Yes, I am.

ADRIA. Good.

JULIO. I handed you a drink earlier this evening.

ADRIA. I don't remember.

JULIO. You were very nice to me.

ADRIA. So, you can be trusted.

JULIO. Absolutely.

ADRIA. Gladys, can he be?

JULIO. I can.

GLADYS. Yes, he can be.

ADRIA. Good.

JULIO. Yes.

ADRIA. Come closer.

JULIO. Can I touch it?

ADRIA. What?

JULIO. The mink coat.

ADRIA. Yes, you can.

THE COOK

JULIO. Black mink! Sweet Jesus!

(JULIO stands by her and touches the coat.)

JULIO. I've only seen pictures of it in Vogue.
GLADYS. You've touched enough.
ADRIA. Hold my hand.
JULIO. What?
GLADYS. Just do it, Julio.
JULIO. Fine.

(JULIO holds her hand.)

JULIO. You're shaking.
GLADYS. You are?
ADRIA. That doesn't matter.
JULIO. Are you sure?
ADRIA. Listen to me!
GLADYS. Listen to her!
JULIO. I am! Jesus!
GLADYS. Don't get so uppity.
JULIO. I'm not.
ADRIA. Just listen.
GLADYS. We are.

(They look at ADRIA.)

ADRIA. Quietly go up to Carlos. Tell him to bring the car to the back alley. He should wait for me there. You're not to say anything to anyone. Either one of you.
JULIO. Yes.
ADRIA. Then continue to hand out the sandwiches.
JULIO. Fine.

THE COOK

GLADYS. Don't you say anything to anyone!
JULIO. I won't.
GLADYS. Take the tray!
JULIO. I will!

(He takes the tray.)

GLADYS. Everything is under control.
JULIO. What a mysterious night.

(JULIO EXITS.)

GLADYS. Is it?
ADRIA. Mysterious?
GLADYS. Yes.
ADRIA. No.
GLADYS. No?
ADRIA. Just factual.
GLADYS. I see. Why are you wearing that coat?
ADRIA. A cold reality has entered the room.
GLADYS. What is it?
ADRIA. What? The material? Didn't you hear your cousin? Mink. It's made out of hundreds of minks. Minks are little furry rat-like animals.
GLADYS. No. The cold reality.
ADRIA. Mink. Black mink.
GLADYS. I never saw it before.
ADRIA. Reality?
GLADYS. The coat.
ADRIA. I bought it in New York.
GLADYS. Is that where you are going?
ADRIA. I don't know.
GLADYS. Please, you can trust me.

ADRIA. I do. I have to.

GLADYS. Has your mother left also?

ADRIA. My mother is vacationing in Barcelona.

GLADYS. I see.

ADRIA. I don't know where I am going, that's why I'm shaking. Can't you see me shake?

GLADYS. Yes! And it breaks my heart.

ADRIA. Oh God! Oh God! I'm scared! Oh God! Jesus! Happy New Year, you bastard. Son of a bitch, Fidel! Help me, Saint Christopher!

GLADYS. I'm sorry.

ADRIA. I do not know where I am going. All I know is I have to leave.

GLADYS. But you know it will be cold.

ADRIA. Yes.

GLADYS. Adria! My Adria! My darling Adria! What's going on?

ADRIA. Chaos.

GLADYS. Is Fidel here?

ADRIA. I imagine he is not in La Habana yet. But he is on his way.

GLADYS. I see.

ADRIA. But my husband called me. I don't know... He called me, told me we must leave.

GLADYS. Say goodbye to your husband for me.

ADRIA. All I know is that Batista has told us to leave. Fidel will march into La Habana tomorrow.

GLADYS. I'm so sorry.

ADRIA. You don't care about me.

GLADYS. I do.

ADRIA. How can you? You work for me.

GLADYS. I do, with all my heart, Adria...

ADRIA. You never called me Adria.

GLADYS. You're leaving and I want to say your name, Adria. Adria. Ah!

ADRIA. Do not let them in here.

THE COOK

GLADYS. I won't.
ADRIA. Fidel's army.
GLADYS. Never.
ADRIA. Fidel's people.
GLADYS. Not while I'm alive. I promise.
ADRIA. Swear it to me!
GLADYS. Over my dead body.
ADRIA. Really?
GLADYS. Trust me.
ADRIA. Maybe you wanted this revolution.
GLADYS. Never.
ADRIA. How can I believe you?
GLADYS. I love my life.
ADRIA. You seem to.
GLADYS. I love my life with you.
ADRIA. Thank you.

(ADRIA goes into her beach bag.)

ADRIA. I hope your cousin is doing his duty,

(GLADYS looks out the door.)

GLADYS. He is. He's serving sandwiches.
ADRIA. Here's five hundred dollars for next month's expenses. Pay the cleaning women. If they ask where I am, say we went on a second honeymoon.
GLADYS. Second honeymoon, in Paris.
ADRIA. Yes, Paris. I like that.
GLADYS. I thought you would.
ADRIA. Second honeymoon, because I am finally pregnant. Tell them I am pregnant.
GLADYS. I'll tell the whole block.

THE COOK

ADRIA. Good. I'll be pregnant in the city of my dreams, Paris.

GLADYS. Wonderful.

ADRIA. So, take five. No, six. You have to pay your cousins.

GLADYS. I'm going to start crying.

ADRIA. You can't.

GLADYS. You'll be back in a month.

ADRIA. I will believe you love me, if you protect my home. If you keep it intact.

GLADYS. I will.

ADRIA. For as long as I'm gone.

GLADYS. Not an ashtray out of place. I promise.

ADRIA. Swear by the Virgin Mary.

GLADYS. I swear.

(We hear laughter and "Happy New Year!")

GLADYS. We couldn't fool them.

ADRIA. The New Year has come. Even in this house where we played with time.

GLADYS. A kiss goodbye.

ADRIA. Yes.

(ADRIA kisses GLADYS on both cheeks.)

ADRIA. Tell them I went to Paris. Not Barcelona.

(ADRIA leaves.)

GLADYS. See you in a month. I'll study the cookbooks. I'll learn to make something that's popular in Paris.

(She goes to a drawer, gets a cigarillo and lights it.)

THE COOK

GLADYS. Happy New Year! Happy New Year!

(JULIO walks in.)

GLADYS. You want one?
JULIO. Sure.
GLADYS. Happy New Year! Happy New Year!
JULIO. Is she gone?
GLADYS. She went to Paris.
JULIO. Really?
GLADYS. Second honeymoon. She's pregnant.
JULIO. They're asking for dessert.
GLADYS. Who?
JULIO. The guests. The people in the party.
GLADYS. I don't care.
JULIO. You don't care?
GLADYS. Tell them their world ended at midnight. Like Cinderella.
JULIO. Fidel won!
GLADYS. Yes.
JULIO. Hallelujah!
GLADYS. You're glad?
JULIO. Yes!
GLADYS. Really, Julio?
JULIO. Of course. And you, Gladys?
GLADYS. I don't know.
JULIO. I guess you'll find out.

(The bell rings.)

JULIO. They are calling for dessert.
GLADYS. What shall we do?
JULIO. Keep smoking?
GLADYS. Why not?

THE COOK

JULIO. The revolution has come.
GLADYS. This part of the revolution, I like.

(The bell rings over and over.)

JULIO. Aggressive.
GLADYS. Yes.
JULIO. The ruling class is like that.
GLADYS. Believe me, I know.
JULIO. They are going to keep calling for dessert all night.

(ELENA ENTERS.)

ELENA. They're mad.

(GLADYS takes the cake pan for the Baked Alaska, hands it to JULIO.)

GLADYS. Let them eat cake.
JULIO. Good.
ELENA. What?
GLADYS. Tell them that the "Baked Alaska" has melted.

(BLACKOUT.)

END OF ACT ONE

ACT II

(El Vedado, Cuba, 1972. The same kitchen. It looks exactly the same, but time has passed. It is a hot, bright summer day. GLADYS is there. She is in her forties. She is dressed in a summer dress that once belonged to Adria. JULIO, her cousin, is talking to her. He is now in his late thirties. He is wearing bell-bottoms, sandals and a T-shirt. He has an Afro. GLADYS is making tamales)

JULIO. Shut the window.

GLADYS. It's hot.

JULIO. Then close the shades.

GLADYS. No.

JULIO. Please.

GLADYS. My eyes aren't as good as they used to be.

JULIO. So...

GLADYS. I need to see what I'm doing.

JULIO. You're making tamales. You can make tamales in the dark.

GLADYS. That's what you think.

JULIO. That's what I know.

GLADYS. I'm getting older.

JULIO. I beg you...

GLADYS. What?

JULIO. Shut the windows and close the shades. Please.

GLADYS. If I do, I'll have to turn on the lights.

JULIO. Who gives a rat's ass?

GLADYS. I do.

JULIO. In a socialist country, you don't have to pay for electricity.

GLADYS. But things wear out.

JULIO. You even want to have light bulbs from 1959.

GLADYS. No. Those burned out in 1961.

JULIO. Close the fucking shades!

THE COOK

GLADYS. Look at this house.

JULIO. No.

GLADYS. The reason why this house looks the same, in this kind of condition, after twelve years... is because I am careful.

JULIO. It's because you are obsessed with the past.

GLADYS. No, I'm not.

JULIO. You're wearing her clothes.

GLADYS. I am sure she wears the latest fashion. Why waste a dress?

JULIO. The style now is above the knee.

GLADYS. I don't care.

JULIO. Your husband is important.

GLADYS. He's sub-minister of transportation. What's the big deal?

JULIO. In a country where everybody takes the bus, and buys gasoline from him...

GLADYS. The government.

JULIO. It's a big deal.

GLADYS. I still have to watch over this house. That's still my job.

JULIO. Do you get paid for it?

GLADYS. There's a blockade. She's not allowed to send me money.

JULIO. I thought she went to Paris.

GLADYS. No.

JULIO. From Europe, you can send money.

GLADYS. Then she's in New York.

JULIO. Do you know this for sure?

GLADYS. No.

(JULIO gives GLADYS a funny look.)

GLADYS. I'm sure she's always thinking about this house, about us.

JULIO. Who gives a fuck?

GLADYS. I do. I waited till last year before I started wearing her dresses.

THE COOK

JULIO. Who gives a fuck about her? She doesn't have to live here! Using everything they left behind till it stops working. Not being able to buy anything new 'cause they don't let anyone but the Russians trade with us... And you're supposed to want to do anything for that rich bitch?

GLADYS. Yes. Don't call her a bitch. You're in her house.

JULIO. It's your house now.

GLADYS. It will always be her house.

JULIO. You sleep in her bedroom.

GLADYS. Only in the summer, because it's cooler.

JULIO. Why do you waste your time?

GLADYS. What do you mean?

JULIO. Saving all of this for her.

GLADYS. I made a vow. I swore to her. I keep my promises.

JULIO. You're obsessed with her. Adria had her mink and she never looked back.

GLADYS. I won't ever believe that.

JULIO. She's never coming back.

GLADYS. She will. Some day, when the blockade ends.

JULIO. All right.

GLADYS. It hurts me when you say stuff like that.

JULIO. Sorry.

GLADYS. Her family was very good to me.

JULIO. I know.

GLADYS. They took a little cleaning girl from Regla and gave her books.

JULIO. Yes, I know.

GLADYS. I had never read a novel till I met her mother.

JULIO. Of course.

GLADYS. They were good to all of us.

JULIO. They treated you like family. I know.

GLADYS. When I married Carlos...

JULIO. They hired him as a chauffeur. I know.

GLADYS. Just like that. To help us.

THE COOK

JULIO. And he took the job.

GLADYS. Yes. Of course.

JULIO. And now he's up there.

GLADYS. Because of the revolution. Without the revolution he'd still be a chauffeur. Pity.

JULIO. You're sorry he got ahead?

GLADYS. Ruined my life.

JULIO. Is that why you wait for Adria?

GLADYS. Adria, on the last day, she told me she was my friend. Can you believe that?

JULIO. It's an easy thing to say when you're exiting.

GLADYS. She meant it.

JULIO. Has she ever written you a letter?

GLADYS. It makes her too sad to write to me.

JULIO. I see. She told you this?

GLADYS. No.

JULIO. When was the last time you had any contact with her?

GLADYS. You know.

JULIO. New Year's Eve, 1958.

GLADYS. Actually, by the time she left, it was 1959. It was past midnight.

JULIO. And time stopped in this kitchen forever.

GLADYS. No.

JULIO. No?

GLADYS. I can feel time pass by.

JULIO. Then why don't you forget her?

GLADYS. I won't.

JULIO. Rich people forget things.

GLADYS. What do you know about rich people?

JULIO. What I read about them from Marx.

GLADYS. Fidel is rich.

JULIO. I know.

GLADYS. He's no saint.

JULIO. He opened schools and didn't expect people to be his servants.

GLADYS. What?

JULIO. He gave little poor girls from Regla the chance to read novels.

GLADYS. The ones he wanted them to read.

JULIO. Just like Adria and her mother.

GLADYS. The reason I didn't hear from her again...

JULIO. Yes.

GLADYS. It's because a wall came down between us. It's called the Iron Curtain.

JULIO. Fine.

GLADYS. You believe me?

JULIO. Yes.

(JULIO looks timidly out the window.)

JULIO. Please, Gladys, please, shut the window.

GLADYS. What?

JULIO. The secret police.

GLADYS. Why?

JULIO. First close the window shades, please.

(GLADYS closes the window shades.)

JULIO. Darkness, comfortable darkness.

GLADYS. There's comfort in sunlight also.

JULIO. For some people.

GLADYS. For decent people.

JULIO. Sometimes I hear El Morro Castle in the dark.

GLADYS. What?

JULIO. At night. Calling me. Telling me, "You will die inside my darkness."

GLADYS. El Morro is a lighthouse.

JULIO. And a jail.

GLADYS. Like everything in this country, it serves two purposes.

JULIO. They take you down a long corridor, with long skinny windows, about three feet apart, looking out into the darkness of the bay. Not the lights of the city.

GLADYS. I had a feeling you were coming today. That's why I started making tamales.

JULIO. Really?

GLADYS. I grated the corn myself, Julio.

JULIO. Carlos didn't help you?

GLADYS. He's too busy being a big shot.

JULIO. Of course.

GLADYS. Big man in the communist party.

JULIO. Yes, he is.

GLADYS. Who would've thought?

JULIO. Many people.

GLADYS. I couldn't tell.

JULIO. You were too busy cooking.

GLADYS. I didn't know how big the change would be.

JULIO. At least you got to keep the house.

GLADYS. Yes.

JULIO. Yes.

GLADYS. Help me make these. Cooking relaxes a...

JULIO. Gladys, take a peek through the shades and see if anyone is looking in.

GLADYS. What?

JULIO. Please.

GLADYS. No.

JULIO. No? Why?

GLADYS. I have to finish making the tamales.

JULIO. Fine.

THE COOK

(JULIO looks.)

JULIO. Fuck! He's still there. This time they mean business. Fuck!

GLADYS. Tamales are all we have left from the indigenous people that once lived here. Their souls comfort us when we eat tamales. And you need comfort, cousin.

JULIO. Yes, I do.

GLADYS. These tamales will bring you peace.

JULIO. I hope you're right.

GLADYS. I know I'm right.

JULIO. Yes?

GLADYS. Yes.

JULIO. Pray for me, cousin.

GLADYS. I'll feed you. That's better than praying.

JULIO. I hope so.

GLADYS. Turn on the lights. I can't see what I'm cooking.

JULIO. Yes.

(JULIO turns on the lights.)

GLADYS. You shouldn't wear such loud clothes.

JULIO. I like them.

GLADYS. Those pants, Julio. No wonder people follow you around.

JULIO. They're in style.

GLADYS. Where? Not here.

JULIO. In the rest of the world.

GLADYS. Not in Russia.

JULIO. No.

GLADYS. Not in China.

JULIO. No.

GLADYS. But in Paris, right?

JULIO. And in the United States.

GLADYS. But not here. And, Julio, you live here.

JULIO. No, not here. Only in a certain crowd.

GLADYS. It's better not to be noticed. Wear them in the privacy of your own house.

JULIO. I always liked style.

GLADYS. I know.

JULIO. You used to give me Adria's old *Vogues*.

GLADYS. Yes, well.

JULIO. You know.

GLADYS. What?

JULIO. I know you know. About me...

GLADYS. Help me stuff the cornhusks, will you?

JULIO. Do you want me to tell you?

GLADYS. You're good at tying the cornhusks together.

JULIO. Do you want me to tell you why I'm being followed?

GLADYS. I went to El Morro Castle once, as a young girl. If you look out from it... to the horizon, you can tell the world is round.

JULIO. Do you?

(Pause.)

GLADYS. Do you need to tell me?

JULIO. What for?

GLADYS. Good.

JULIO. I think there's a part of you that knows already. You know about me.

GLADYS. I know you're my cousin and I love you.

JULIO. What else?

GLADYS. What?

JULIO. What else have you heard?

GLADYS. Nothing.

JULIO. Liar.

GLADYS. I don't like to listen to malicious rumors about my family.

JULIO. Maybe sometimes you should.

GLADYS. Stop being lazy and help me.

JULIO. Listen to me. Some things are rumors. Some things are facts.

GLADYS. So what?

JULIO. Fact: I never got married.

GLADYS. Fact: you never found the right girl.

JULIO. Fact: I don't know how to love a woman.

GLADYS. Fact: your first girlfriend broke your heart.

JULIO. Fact: the secret police are after me because of my improper conduct.

GLADYS. Because your pants are too tight?

JULIO. Much more.

GLADYS. Improper conduct is when a person behaves outside the norm.

JULIO. When did this country become so moralistic?

GLADYS. When Raul Castro went to China... and he asked how they handled their homosexual problem. They replied, "We kill them, throw them in the river and then let their bodies float down to town. So they can see what the punishment is for improper conduct." But Cuba, being more humanistic, just puts deviants in camps.

JULIO. So you're aware of what goes on in the world.

GLADYS. Yes I am.

JULIO. Good.

GLADYS. Why?

JULIO. So you can understand.

GLADYS. What?

JULIO. Me.

GLADYS. You?

JULIO. I'm a deviant.

GLADYS. Marry someone.

JULIO. I can't.

GLADYS. Why not?

JULIO. Because I have fallen in love.

GLADYS. I see.
JULIO. And his family...
GLADYS. You've fallen in love with a man?
JULIO. He's almost a man.
GLADYS. Almost is not the same thing.
JULIO. For me it is.
GLADYS. Is he white?
JULIO. Yes.
GLADYS. Marry someone.
JULIO. No.
GLADYS. Save yourself.

(CARLOS walks in. He has a beard now, which is graying. He wears a suit.)

CARLOS. Julio.
JULIO. Yes, Carlos.
CARLOS. Have you joined the Navy?
JULIO. Why do you say that, Carlos?
CARLOS. No man would wear pants like that for any other reason.
JULIO. I haven't joined the Navy.
CARLOS. Or have you just been visiting the docks?
GLADYS. Carlos, leave Julio alone.
CARLOS. Really?
GLADYS. Really.
CARLOS. I can say whatever I want, in my house.
GLADYS. If you had one.
CARLOS. Had what?
GLADYS. A house.
CARLOS. I do.
GLADYS. Really?
CARLOS. Yes.
GLADYS. Where?

THE COOK

CARLOS. Here. This is my house.

GLADYS. Really. You're full of fairy tales today!

CARLOS. The government gave it to me as a gift.

GLADYS. Was it theirs to give?

CARLOS. What do you mean?

GLADYS. The owner of the house put me in charge of it.

CARLOS. This house belongs to the people.

GLADYS. Aren't I the people?

CARLOS. You're no longer the boss.

GLADYS. I was never the boss.

CARLOS. Really?

GLADYS. Really! Absolutely. No doubt in my mind!

CARLOS. Funny, that's not how I remember it.

JULIO. Your memory is selective, Carlos.

CARLOS. What do you mean by that?

JULIO. You forget that you were without a job before you married my cousin. And then suddenly, like magic, you had a uniform and became a chauffeur.

CARLOS. Don't start fucking around with me, Julio. If you know what's good for you.

JULIO. All right.

CARLOS. Good.

GLADYS. Big man in town now.

CARLOS. Yes I am. You should be proud.

GLADYS. I would be if you hadn't betrayed me.

CARLOS. Betrayal is in the eye of the beholder. Truth is sometimes called betrayal.

GLADYS. And adultery?

CARLOS. A way of life.

GLADYS. Ah.

(GLADYS makes the tamales.)

THE COOK

GLADYS. You cheat on me with someone younger and I'm supposed to think that's revolutionary also.

CARLOS. I got the memory of an elephant. I know how much shit I had to swallow before the revolution.

JULIO. How do you remember it, Carlos?

GLADYS. Incorrectly, that's how he remembers it.

CARLOS. I do no think so.

GLADYS. I know so.

CARLOS. I remember that you were a totalitarian in this kitchen,

GLADYS. And with good reason.

CARLOS. And all you care about, and all you know about is this house, this corner of El Vedado. Do you have any idea what's going on outside?

GLADYS. Charity from the Russians.

JULIO. See? More than you thought, Carlos.

CARLOS. Charity from the Russians. Is that all you see?

GLADYS. Yes.

CARLOS. No. You stupid bitch! The people's revolution, that's what's going on outside this house. That's what's going on in this country. There's a dialectical explosion going on. It has rocked the world. We've said no to capitalism. No to the class system. That's what's going on. And there's no room for a dictator, not even in a kitchen. And that's why you hate me... 'Cause now I'm your equal.

GLADYS. Equal? No.

CARLOS. Yes. Not the guy you got a job for. I'm part of the greatest revolution on the face of this earth.

JULIO. Really, Carlos?

GLADYS. There are a million Cubans in Miami that disagree with you.

CARLOS. Who the hell do you know in Miami?

GLADYS. People.

CARLOS. Name them.

GLADYS. Never mind...

THE COOK

JULIO. I'll answer for you.

CARLOS. You're talking for her now.

JULIO. Well, for example....

CARLOS. Yes?

GLADYS. The people who own this house.

JULIO. That's right.

GLADYS. Adria Santana and her husband, Pablo. And whatever child they had.

CARLOS. Will you ever evolve beyond this kitchen?

GLADYS. I have evolved...

CARLOS. Really?

GLADYS. Yes. I no longer sleep with you.

JULIO. That's right.

CARLOS. Personal, sexual politics, still bourgeois.

JULIO. Really?

GLADYS. The emancipation of the female is not a bourgeois concept. It's revolutionary. Anarchistic, even.

JULIO. Good for you, cousin.

CARLOS. You guard this house like the sphinx at the pyramids.

GLADYS. I keep my promises, my vows.

CARLOS. Then be a wife.

GLADYS. I wash your clothes, I feed you. I even care about you. I just don't love you anymore.

JULIO. You broke her heart.

CARLOS. No.

JULIO. You cheated on her.

CARLOS. But I did not break her heart.

JULIO. What?

CARLOS. My cheating was a reaction to her broken heart.

GLADYS. Liar.

CARLOS. No.

JULIO. You are.

CARLOS. No. Adria. Adria Santana broke her heart. She never came

THE COOK

back.
JULIO. Oh.
GLADYS. She will.

(CARLOS sneaks a look out the window.)

JULIO. He's still out there.
CARLOS. Who?
GLADYS. Don't tell him anything.
CARLOS. Tell me.
JULIO. Well...
GLADYS. Don't.
JULIO. Maybe he can help me.
GLADYS. No.
CARLOS. Come on.
JULIO. Someone from the secret police has been following me.
CARLOS. 'Cause you are a faggot!
JULIO. Yes, because I'm a faggot.
CARLOS. With pants like the ones you have on, what else could you be?
JULIO. I have the right to wear whatever I want.
CARLOS. You do not.
JULIO. Yes, I do.
GLADYS. Julio, Carlos is right. For once he's right. Why show your weakness?
JULIO. Because it's not a weakness.
CARLOS. See the problem we're faced with...?
JULIO. What?
CARLOS. A society that can't be weak. Do you see that Gladys?
JULIO. Don't answer.
GLADYS. Go upstairs. To the master bedroom.
CARLOS. The one you keep me out of.
GLADYS. Because you have a mistress.

THE COOK

CARLOS. A man like me has a right to a mistress.

JULIO. I'm the one in trouble.

GLADYS. Yes. And I'm going to get you out of it.

CARLOS. Are you?

GLADYS. Listen to me, Julio. In her husband's closet. You know which one that is.

CARLOS. The one on the right hand side of the room.

GLADYS. The one to the left of the bathroom. In it, there are many proper pants and shirts and shoes. Take one of each. Put them on. I'm going to let you borrow them. So they won't know it's you, when you leave this house.

CARLOS. Also a hat.

GLADYS. Yes, a Panama.

CARLOS. Stick all that fucking hair into it.

JULIO. He was bigger then me.

CARLOS. Wear a belt.

GLADYS. Belts are in the chest of drawers by the window.

JULIO. I'll look fat in his clothes.

GLADYS. You will look like a man.

CARLOS. Do it quickly, Julio. You're the only person she has ever given anything to, from this holy place.

JULIO. Gladys?

GLADYS. Do it!

JULIO. I'll be back.

(JULIO EXITS.)

GLADYS. Will you help him?

CARLOS. He parades himself in every part of town.

GLADYS. I need you to help him.

CARLOS. He's having an affair with an eighteen-year-old white boy, whose father works at the Ministry of Information.

GLADYS. Is his father trusted by the party?

CARLOS. His character is questionable.
GLADYS. Then save my cousin.
CARLOS. Fine.
GLADYS. Thank you.
CARLOS. We're still family.
GLADYS. Yes.
CARLOS. He's gonna have to start behaving differently.
GLADYS. I'll speak to his mother.
CARLOS. Tamales! Will you let me eat as many as I want?
GLADYS. Yes.
CARLOS. Well.
GLADYS. All of them, if you want.
CARLOS. You're really grateful.
GLADYS. Yes, I am.
CARLOS. Finally.
GLADYS. You have me where you want me.
CARLOS. I still love you.
GLADYS. You should.

(GLADYS starts to cook the tamales. Throwing the wrapped ones into a pot of boiling water.)

CARLOS. There is one thing.
GLADYS. Yes.
CARLOS. Family...
GLADYS. Yes.
CARLOS. I have another, as you know.
GLADYS. Yes.
CARLOS. And it's getting larger.
GLADYS. You have two mistresses now?
CARLOS. No.
GLADYS. Then?
CARLOS. Well...

GLADYS. Yes?

CARLOS. My girlfriend is pregnant.

GLADYS. Bastard!

CARLOS. Come on.

GLADYS. You cheating bastard!

CARLOS. Yes, I am.

GLADYS. I hate you. I hate you. I hate you. God, I hate you!

CARLOS. So I guess it was you who wasn't fertile.

GLADYS. Maybe she cheated on you.

CARLOS. Never.

GLADYS. Sure of yourself.

CARLOS. That girl worships me.

GLADYS. Or your position.

CARLOS. My position is me.

GLADYS. True. Why can't I stop hating you?

CARLOS. Unrequited passion.

GLADYS. Passion? Do not flatter yourself.

CARLOS. All right.

GLADYS. Please. Passion? Please.

CARLOS. I want her to move in here. I want my child to live in the best I can give.

GLADYS. You're nuts.

CARLOS. I think we could all live in my house together.

GLADYS. This is not your house.

CARLOS. I tried to find her another place. But finding housing is impossible in La Habana.

GLADYS. Even for an important man like you?

CARLOS. Yes.

GLADYS. Or are you just a third-tier Fidelista?

CARLOS. Powerful enough to have somebody put away.

GLADYS. Like my cousin.

CARLOS. Put in a camp.

GLADYS. You would do that?

CARLOS. Yes, I would.

GLADYS. If I don't give you what you want.

CARLOS. That's right.

GLADYS. You think you can threaten me.

CARLOS. I'm asking you to be logical.

GLADYS. This house is for Adria. I take care of it. I don't want your brat and your girlfriend bringing their filth into this place.

CARLOS. You know you're being stupid. The only reason we live alone in this house. The only reason any other family has not moved in. Is because of me. My power, my influence. Favors I've asked for. That's why you live in this house. Because of me...admit it.

GLADYS. I have my pride.

CARLOS. If you don't do this...

GLADYS. You won't lift a finger to help him.

CARLOS. I will point the finger to destroy him.

GLADYS. What are you?

CARLOS. A man who can do in his castle whatever he wants.

GLADYS. Really?

CARLOS. Yes. I'm the boss here.

GLADYS. Not while I'm alive.

CARLOS. Is that your answer?

GLADYS. Point the finger, Carlos.

CARLOS. Bitch.

GLADYS. And live with the guilt.

CARLOS. Stupid, stupid girl.

GLADYS. Proud woman.

CARLOS. You'll never learn.

(CARLOS leaves.)

GLADYS. Cook, Gladys. Cook.

(She puts the tamales into a pot. CARLOS walks back in.)

THE COOK

CARLOS. I just told your cousin how you betrayed him.
GLADYS. I'm not betraying myself for any man.
CARLOS. You're black. Do you know that?
GLADYS. Yes. I do.
CARLOS. You're not her.
GLADYS. Yes I know.

(CARLOS leaves.)

GLADYS. But in her house, in her clothes, I feel like I am.

(JULIO walks in.)

JULIO. How could you?
GLADYS. Run out into the streets, Julio. Try to get on a raft. When you get to Miami, Adria will help you.
JULIO. Carlos could've saved me.
GLADYS. Save yourself.
JULIO. But...
GLADYS. No more buts.
JULIO. I need...
GLADYS. No more words.
JULIO. You can't...
GLADYS. No words. Run.
JULIO. I...
GLADYS. Save yourself.
JULIO. I don't know how.
GLADYS. Go.
JULIO. I'm scared.
GLADYS. Stop it.
JULIO. I'm scared.
GLADYS. Be a man.

THE COOK

JULIO. They won't let me.

GLADYS. Get out!

JULIO. I want to eat dinner first.

GLADYS. They'll be coming after you soon.

JULIO. Tell Carlos that you're sorry.

GLADYS. But I'm not.

JULIO. You won't save me.

GLADYS. No.

JULIO. You never loved me.

GLADYS. Sometimes there are things bigger than love.

JULIO. I hate you.

GLADYS. Fine.

JULIO. You could've helped me.

GLADYS. By now Carlos is pointing the finger at you. Go.

JULIO. But...

GLADYS. No more meals here.

JULIO. God!

GLADYS. You should've married somebody.

JULIO. I thought the revolution was also going to include me.

GLADYS. You were wrong.

JULIO. God!

GLADYS. Get out of my kitchen.

JULIO. Yes.

GLADYS. Go to Miami.

JULIO. Sure.

GLADYS. Adria will help you.

JULIO. You could've saved me.

GLADYS. The tamales are going to get overcooked.

(JULIO leaves.)

GLADYS. Adria!

THE COOK

(We hear a police siren.)

You see? I kept my word, Adria. But will you ever be back?

(She opens one of the tamales and tries to eat it.)

GLADYS. Too much salt.

(She takes another taste.)

GLADYS. No. Bitter. The corn must have been bitter. Not my fault. Not my fault.

(BLACKOUT.)

END OF ACT TWO

ACT III

(The kitchen, 1997. The kitchen still looks the same. But it has now faded with time. It is lunchtime. Gladys has turned the house into a "paladar" — the Cuban word for a restaurant inside a private home. Gladys is now in her seventies, but still looks good and younger than she is. She is dressed extremely well. Carlos is wearing a white apron and is chopping onions. His daughter Rosa, a dark skinned girl in her twenties, is chopping garlic)

CARLOS. It's getting to be more and more work.

GLADYS. What is?

CARLOS. This cooking business.

GLADYS. Thank God.

ROSA. They all want Gladys' garlic chicken.

GLADYS. Good.

CARLOS. Why?

GLADYS. It's an easy thing to make. Just lots of oranges, limes, garlic, onions and some oregano. And then put it in the oven.

ROSA. You're right.

GLADYS. An easy way to make dollars.

CARLOS. It's not so we can make dollars, it's so we can survive.

ROSA. I want to do more than survive.

CARLOS. Careful daughter. You're talking like a capitalist.

GLADYS. So? Where would we be without the tourists' dollars?

CARLOS. Living on my pension.

GLADYS. You mean starving on your pension?

CARLOS. We're a socialist society. We take care of each other.

GLADYS. With tourists and dollars.

CARLOS. Its all the blockade's fault.

GLADYS. It's all Fidel Castro's fault.

CARLOS. No it's not. The blockade made him dependent on the

Russians. When the Russians abandoned us, we came to this special period...

GLADYS. Of starvation?

CARLOS. What?

GLADYS. You heard me.

CARLOS. We're not starving.

GLADYS. Because of my cooking and the beauty of this house.

ROSA. You have to admit she's right.

CARLOS. She doesn't have to be arrogant.

GLADYS. Proud.

(CARLOS looks inside a small notebook.)

CARLOS. How many reservations so far today?

ROSA. Ten for lunch.

CARLOS. Good. We're meeting our goals.

ROSA. Yes we are!

CARLOS. I knew we would.

GLADYS. Now, who's become a capitalist?

CARLOS. In this special period, we all have to change our way of surviving, but not our ideals.

GLADYS. What did your ideals get you?

CARLOS. Dignity.

GLADYS. And a city that is falling apart.

CARLOS. Fidel feels terrible about it.

GLADYS. He told you this?

CARLOS. The last time I talked with Fidel was thirty years ago.

GLADYS. At a gathering you took her mother to.

CARLOS. You were anti-communist.

GLADYS. Was that the reason?

CARLOS. You know it was.

GLADYS. Fine.

CARLOS. If Fidel says bring the tourists back...

THE COOK

ROSA. Then why not feed them, right Papi?

CARLOS. Right.

GLADYS. You, Carlos, should thank God and the Virgin Mother of Regla that I can still cook at my age.

CARLOS. So, ten reservations.

ROSA. Yes, as of this moment.

CARLOS. And there will be people that will just walk in.

ROSA. That's what always happens.

CARLOS. Yes.

GLADYS. And it's film festival time, don't forget that.

ROSA. I should have my camera ready.

GLADYS. Yes, you should.

CARLOS. I love having my picture taken with movie stars.

ROSA. We know you do.

GLADYS. Rosa, buy more film next time you're at the Nacional.

ROSA. I will, Gladys.

(The bell rings.)

CARLOS. Somebody's here early.

GLADYS. No one's rung that bell in more than thirty years.

CARLOS. What are you saying?

GLADYS. That no one's rung the bell in more than...

CARLOS. Must be Spaniards. They're always hungry.

(The bell rings.)

GLADYS. Aggressive.

CARLOS. Then, they're German.

ROSA. I'll get it.

GLADYS. Remember, today we have chicken, lobster, pork, plantains and rum flavored ice cream.

ROSA. Rum.

CARLOS. Yum!

ROSA. Keep your hands away from it, papi.

CARLOS. I will.

ROSA. Promise.

CARLOS. I promise.

ROSA. Gladys, the day you decided to turn this place into a paladar...

GLADYS. I wish we could call it a restaurant.

ROSA. That's the day I knew you had genius in you.

GLADYS. Thank you, sweet girl.

CARLOS. Restaurants are run by the government, not individuals.

GLADYS. Part of the insanity.

CARLOS. The logic of revolution.

GLADYS. It's a good thing I figured out a way around the revolutionary logic.

ROSA. We are one of the first paladars.

CARLOS. Always thought she should've been a chef.

GLADYS. Did you? Did you really? Carlos!

CARLOS. You know I did.

GLADYS. You never helped me get out of this house.

CARLOS. Don't start.

(The bell rings.)

ROSA. I better take care of the customers.

GLADYS. You do that, sweetie.

(ROSA leaves.)

GLADYS. Good girl.

CARLOS. I knew we'd be one happy family. But I had to wait till her mother died.

GLADYS. Her mother did not die. She went to Miami.

CARLOS. Dead to me.

THE COOK

GLADYS. You should forgive the ones that left.

CARLOS. Never!

GLADYS. Why not?

CARLOS. The blockade.

GLADYS. Are you going to be a communist till the day you die?

CARLOS. Yes I am.

GLADYS. Even though they never gave you what they promised you.

CARLOS. They tried.

GLADYS. How?

CARLOS. I know they tried. But the blockade...

GLADYS. You'll never learn.

CARLOS. That's why I still love you.

GLADYS. Sure.

CARLOS. I will always love you for taking my Rosa in.

GLADYS. She's a sweet girl.

CARLOS. You raised her.

GLADYS. Yes, I did.

CARLOS. That's why she's a great worker.

GLADYS. Yes, she is.

CARLOS. Yes, she is.

GLADYS. Adria would've liked her.

CARLOS. I wouldn't have let my daughter work for Adria.

GLADYS. Only your wife?

CARLOS. I didn't like you working for her either. But we had no other choice back then.

GLADYS. We have no other choice now.

CARLOS. What are you talking about?

GLADYS. They're all coming back. And we wait on them. Tourists. What's changed?

CARLOS. My daughter is studying to be an engineer and this is our place.

GLADYS. Maybe.

CARLOS. That's a big difference. And Cuba belongs to us.

GLADYS. The proletarians?

CARLOS. Yes.

GLADYS. Well...

CARLOS. Did you like anything about the revolution?

GLADYS. Yes. I liked that we remained Cuban. During Batista, we were becoming something else.

CARLOS. Now we are who we are.

GLADYS. Yes we are.

CARLOS. That's right. I love Fidel. I love the man.

GLADYS. With your lousy pension.

CARLOS. I would have understood hunger...

GLADYS. You never liked being hungry Carlos.

CARLOS. But I didn't think he'd ever willingly let them back in.

GLADYS. The ones that left?

CARLOS. Yes. The traitors. The worms.

GLADYS. He needs their dollars. We need their dollars.

CARLOS. Not fair.

GLADYS. We always have needed their dollars.

CARLOS. Fuck them.

GLADYS. Can't live without rich people, if you want to eat well.

CARLOS. I think now there's a chance that Adria will come back.

(Pause)

GLADYS. Really?

CARLOS. Isn't that what you've been hoping for.

GLADYS. It would be the answer to my prayers.

CARLOS. Are you crazy?

GLADYS. She'd see that I kept my word; that I was faithful.

CARLOS. Jesus fucking Christ!

GLADYS. Why are you cursing Christ when you denied his existence for forty years? Why don't you say Karl fucking Marx?

THE COOK

(GLADYS laughs.)

CARLOS. This is not a joke.

GLADYS. It all seems funny to me.

CARLOS. What would happen to your business? What would happen to our lives? They'd want the house back. We'd starve.

GLADYS. No, she'd give me a better pension then the one that Fidel gave you.

CARLOS. You're a fool.

GLADYS. No I'm not. I know what people I can trust.

CARLOS. I don't want them coming here and taking away everything I earned.

GLADYS. Serves you right.

CARLOS. You really hate me, don't you?

GLADYS. Let them take what belongs to them. If they come back, I'll give it to them.

(Pause)

CARLOS. Well... I think they will.

GLADYS. Does that scare you?

CARLOS. Why should it? I never betrayed her.

GLADYS. No.

CARLOS. I just survived after they deserted us.

GLADYS. Yes.

CARLOS. Yes.

(ROSA walks in.)

GLADYS. So, what's the order?

CARLOS. Come on. I'm ready.

ROSA. She's not sure she wants lunch.

THE COOK

GLADYS. Then why is she here? One comes here to eat.

ROSA. She just wants to take pictures.

GLADYS. We're not a museum.

CARLOS. Is she German?

ROSA. No.

GLADYS. French?

ROSA. No.

GLADYS. Canadian?

CARLOS. Italian?

ROSA. From the U.S. But she walks like a Cuban and her husband is a gringo.

GLADYS. A couple.

ROSA. Yes.

GLADYS. Tell them they can't take pictures. Without ordering food.

ROSA. What?

GLADYS. They can take pictures, if they buy lunch. If they don't, then, no pictures.

ROSA. They seem nice.

GLADYS. No dollars, no pictures.

ROSA. What's the harm?

GLADYS. This is not a tourist site.

ROSA. But...

CARLOS. Gladys is right.

ROSA. Fine.

CARLOS. I'll go tell them.

ROSA. No, I will.

(The bell rings.)

CARLOS. Uppity.

ROSA. Yes.

GLADYS. She must be Cuban-American.

ROSA. Must be.

THE COOK

GLADYS. Is she wearing a lot of jewelry?
ROSA. No.
GLADYS. No? Now, that's odd.
CARLOS. Yes. They usually look like a walking jewelry store.
GLADYS. I hear they rent them, so they can show up looking rich.
CARLOS. That's also what I hear.

(The bell rings.)

ROSA. I better go.

(ROSA leaves.)

GLADYS. I think you're not chopping the onions fine enough.
CARLOS. Yes, I am.
GLADYS. A little finer, please.
CARLOS. So we've come full circle, haven't we?
GLADYS. What do you mean?
CARLOS. You get to boss me around in the kitchen again.
GLADYS. Yes.
CARLOS. You like it?
GLADYS. Yes, I do.
CARLOS. I thought so.

(ROSA walks in.)

GLADYS. So?
ROSA. She wants to take pictures of the bedrooms, the bathrooms and the kitchen.
GLADYS. Who the hell does she think she is?
ROSA. She said she owns this place.
GLADYS. She's back.
CARLOS. Oh, my God!

GLADYS. How do I look? Oh my God! Adria!

ROSA. No, that her family owned this place.

CARLOS. Ssshhhh.

GLADYS. Bring her in here.

ROSA. Are you sure?

GLADYS. Positive.

(ROSA EXITS.)

CARLOS. It's happened.

GLADYS. Thank you, sweet Mary.

CARLOS. The world has gone around and come back in the same direction.

(LOURDES, ADRIA's daughter, walks in. She looks exactly like ADRIA. She has a camera. She is taking pictures.)

LOURDES. My god! I recognize it all, even the hallway in front of the kitchen.

ROSA. She has worked hard to keep it the same.

GLADYS. Sometimes miracles do happen.

CARLOS. My God!

GLADYS. What?

CARLOS. Look at her. She hasn't aged. Look at us. We have.

LOURDES. My mother, she kept it all alive in her mind. And I guess I remember more of her stories than I thought. That's interesting. I was listening after all.

ROSA. The kitchen is right in here.

LOURDES. My god. I'm beginning to understand how much she really lost. It's so beautiful here.

ROSA. Yes it is.

GLADYS. Come into the kitchen. Please.

THE COOK

(LOURDES walks up to GLADYS,)

GLADYS. I kept it the same for your return. Forty years, Adria. And I kept it clean and in order for you.

LOURDES. Who are you?

GLADYS. I've gotten old. I know. I'm sorry. I'm the cook.

LOURDES. The cook?

GLADYS. Oh my God! She doesn't recognize me. How can you not recognize me?

LOURDES. The cook and the chauffeur. Is that who you are?

GLADYS. Yes.

LOURDES. I see. What do you know. Who would have thought you'd still be here?

GLADYS. Look at us. We waited for you.

LOURDES. Yes. (She goes up to Rosa) Listen, thank you for showing me the house. Very nice of you. But I think I better go.

ROSA. Really, so soon?

LOURDES. I'm not really ready for this. I'm getting a little angry and I don't know why.

ROSA. There is nothing to be angry about.

LOURDES. Don't be naive.

ROSA. I'm not naive. There is nothing to be angry about.

LOURDES. What do you mean? There are decades of dictatorship to be angry about.

ROSA. Revolution.

LOURDES. What?

ROSA. Decades of revolution.

LOURDES. Right. Sorry.

CARLOS. You recognize us now?

LOURDES. Yes I do.

GLADYS. Thank god!

LOURDES. You are the people who my mother told me about.

GLADYS. Adria?

LOURDES. Yes. She told me.

ROSA. She's the daughter. Gladys. Adria's daughter.

GLADYS. The daughter. She had a daughter! I'm so happy. You look just like her. As beautiful as Adria. What's your name dear?

LOURDES. Lourdes.

GLADYS. After your great Aunt.

LOURDES. Yes that's right. I never met her. She died here.

GLADYS. She did. She did die here. Around nineteen sixty six.....In August. August 31, 1966. That's right. Sometimes I think she died of loneliness. After everyone left, I tried to visit her every once in a while. But she stopped opening the door. I tried to explain to her that I was not a communist, but well....I'm afraid her mind had gone a little. Just like her mother's....your great grandmother Soraya....like mother like daughter....

LOURDES. You know my heritage?

GLADYS. Like the back of my hand. Oh my God. Look at you sweet little Lourdes. So brave to come all the way here and visit us. Isn't she brave Carlos?

CARLOS. I don't know.

GLADYS. Sit down. Carlos get her husband. Maybe we should go into the living room? You want some water, mango juice?

CARLOS. Rum?

LOURDES. I don't think so. You are being so friendly and you did....

ROSA. We are very friendly.

CARLOS. We don't have a blockade against you.

(CARLOS EXIT.)

LOURDES. I don't really know any of you. Thank you for showing me the house. I just needed to see the house.

GLADYS. If you had been born here, you would have known me as well as you know your mother.

LOURDES. But I wasn't born here.

THE COOK

GLADYS. That's the tragedy.

LOURDES. I don't think so. Maybe for my mother but not for me. She felt so betrayed by everyone that stayed.

GLADYS. Not by me?

LOURDES. By everyone that stayed.

GLADYS. Please believe me, I did not betray her.

LOURDES. That's not what she believes.

GLADYS. What does she think? Tell me. Please!

LOURDES. That you were communists all along...

GLADYS. We were not!

LOURDES. You had been plotting all along.

GLADYS. What?

LOURDES. To take her house and keep it for yourselves.

GLADYS. I was not! Never. I never had a thought like that! Never! She was my best friend. I knew her when we were both girls. How could I ever? Ever even think of harming....

LOURDES. That you lied to her.

GLADYS. Lied to her? I worshipped your mother.

LOURDES. Really?

GLADYS. Really.

ROSA. She talks about her every day. She's been waiting for forty years for her return.

LOURDES. I don't know what to believe. It's a confusing country.

ROSA. No, it's a simple country.

GLADYS. No, it's not!

LOURDES. You agree with me?

GLADYS. Yes, must be hard to come back here, dear.

LOURDES. I was never here.

GLADYS. Right.

LOURDES. I'm an American

ROSA. Are you?

LOURDES. Yes. I'm not my mother. I can forgive.

GLADYS. You can forgive me?

THE COOK

LOURDES. Can I take a picture?

GLADYS. It's your house.

LOURDES. You really feel that way?

GLADYS. I've been waiting to give it back.

LOURDES. That's stretching it.

GLADYS. Why?

LOURDES. Look, it's easy to say you want to give it back. When there is no way to give it back. And you know it. There is no way that we could come back here to live...

ROSA. Because of the blockade.

LOURDES. Because of Fidel Castro. So the house is yours. Really. You took it. You lived in it. Not me. So please, just let me take a few pictures to take back to my mother. She'll cry over them. And hate you just a little bit more.

GLADYS. Hate me? Please tell her that I....

LOURDES. She won't want to know anything about you. Believe me. And really, how can you blame her?

GLADYS. I had nothing to do with the revolution.

LOURDES. To my mother, you are the revolution.

ROSA. She made sacrifices and cut corners to make sure it got a fresh coat of paint once in a while. Their marriage was ruined over it...Her cousin died in a camp because of it.

GLADYS. No, my cousin died in a camp because of us.

GLADYS. Lourdes?

LOURDES. Yes?

GLADYS. Give me a moment. I deserve a moment..

LOURDES. Fine. *(Pause.)* Yes?

GLADYS. I worked for your family since I was thirteen years old. My name is Gladys.

LOURDES. They never mentioned your name, I mean.

GLADYS. So I am telling you my name. My name is Gladys.

LOURDES. Well...hello Gladys. Thank you for this glimpse into my mother. But I really should go.

THE COOK

GLADYS. How is your father?

LOURDES. He passed away.

GLADYS. How?

LOURDES. I don't think I have to answer that.

GLADYS. Please.

LOURDES. I'm trying. I really am trying. But I am getting so angry. It's irrational, isn't it? I don't like being irrational. But this whole Cuba thing is like a god damned tornado. I didn't think that I would be so angry. But...This should have been mine. My house. My life.

ROSA. But your mother decided to leave.

LOURDES. She had no choice.

ROSA. Perhaps.

GLADYS. She was scared. The revolution was against the people like her. But nobody knew that then. I didn't know that.

LOURDES. Maybe you did, maybe you didn't. But you sure have lived well, off my parents' misfortune.

ROSA. She only stayed in this house to save it for your mother. Tell your mother that.

GLADYS. Please. Yes, tell her that. Good, Rosa. Thank you Rosa.

ROSA. Anytime Gladys. So you'll tell her.

LOURDES. The conversation would only get as far as I went to the house and I met the cook, then she would walk away...

GLADYS. I loved Adria.

LOURDES. My mother is a very angry woman. Her only thought is revenge.

GLADYS. Against me?

LOURDES. Against anyone who stayed behind. She hasn't spoken to me for the past month, because I was coming here.

ROSA. Miami Mafia.

GLADYS. Be quiet Rosa.

LOURDES. This can't have a happy ending. I should go.

ROSA. What made you come?

LOURDES. Well...unfinished business...but my husband... He is sort

THE COOK

of a ... well, a Democrat... He thought I should come and see my mother's world.

ROSA. You should.

GLADYS. Look at me then.

LOURDES. Why?

GLADYS. I was your mother's world.

LOURDES. And she never ever mentioned you by name. She's so bitter. Do you know what it was like to live with someone who became so bitter?

ROSA. How did your father die?

LOURDES. What?

ROSA. You owe her that much.

LOURDES. Do I really?

ROSA. Yes!

LOURDES. I wasn't born here.

GLADYS. You were conceived here.

LOURDES. Really?

GLADYS. Yes, I remember the day your mother told me. New Year's Eve, 1958. I was in the kitchen. We were throwing a big party...I was making lime ice cream. She held my hand and told me. We were that close. She told me before she told your father. That's how much we meant to each other. That's the night she left. The night she asked me to keep this place the same for her. Till she returned. Haven't I done a good job? Lourdes?

LOURDES. My father died in Africa. They were there protecting some of Batista's oil interests. He died in her arms after his birthday party in 1972. She even blames that on Fidel.

ROSA. She should blame Batista. Why doesn't anyone blame Batista for anything?

LOURDES. Well...

ROSA. Do you believe us?

LOURDES. Yes I think so. I feel terrible. I feel like I'm betraying her now. If I understand you. I betray her. You see? I should go.

THE COOK

GLADYS. Where does she live now?

LOURDES. In East Hampton. She married again.

GLADYS. Good.

LOURDES. I don't want to end up like her.

GLADYS. How?

LOURDES. Doing nothing with my life.

(CARLOS walks back in.)

CARLOS. Your husband is waiting for you in the car.

GLADYS. He doesn't want to have lunch?

CARLOS. I don't think so.

LOURDES. He's like that.

ROSA. We're a very famous paladar. We're in all the guidebooks.

GLADYS. It would be on the house.

CARLOS. For sure.

LOURDES. Thank you, but...

ROSA. A free meal.

LOURDES. I can't.

GLADYS. Please.

LOURDES. My husband is very picky about food. He thinks in third world countries you should only eat at the hotels.

ROSA. Ah, well. Not that liberal. I should have guessed.

LOURDES. He tries.

ROSA. And you?

LOURDES. I don't think I can be a guest at my mother's house. Eat at the table that was stolen from her. I can't go that far. I'm sorry.

ROSA. I see.

LOURDES. Gladys, would you like me to take a picture of you to give my mother?

GLADYS. No.

LOURDES. Why not?

GLADYS. I'm not a tourist attraction.

THE COOK

LOURDES. You're not? You're in the guide books.

GLADYS. No. I'm not.

CARLOS. Is your mother still rich?

LOURDES. Not as rich as she was here.

CARLOS. Good.

LOURDES. My family worked hard for their money. Don't insult them.

ROSA. But you are.

LOURDES. What?

ROSA. Insulting.

LOURDES. I don't think I am. Just because I won't eat here. That makes me insulting.

ROSA. No. Because you do not see the history you are facing.

LOURDES. It's not my history. I want nothing to do with my mother's history.

ROSA. Liar! You came here with your mind made up and you can not face the fact that we are not what you expected.

CARLOS. The ruling class always looks the other way. Remember that, daughter. They treat us well, when it's convenient for them. You won't accept what we are willing to give you.

LOURDES. And what's that?

CARLOS. We are offering you love.

LOURDES. Do you love me, or my money?

ROSA. How can you say that? Do you have no humanity? Is that what happens in the United States?

LOURDES. This is not about me. This is about how you can not survive without the dollar.

ROSA. No. It is about you. It is about you and me. How to deal with the past. So we can live in the present. So we can have a future. What's going on here has nothing to do with dollars. Don't you see?

LOURDES. I think it does. You used my mother's house, my mother's past. The most precious part of her memories, her youth, her home. You took it and you turned it into a restaurant. I'm surprised you didn't turn it into a brothel.

GLADYS. Get out of my house!

LOURDES. Your house?

GLADYS. Yes, my history, my house!

LOURDES. So that's what you really think. My mother was right.

GLADYS. Not until today.

LOURDES. What?

GLADYS. I didn't think this was my house, until I met you.

LOURDES. Well...

GLADYS. Leave me alone. God, I was a fool. Get out of here.

LOURDES. My mother said, "Imagine my house, my bathroom, my bed, being lived in, slept on, by a bunch of niggers."

ROSA. You arrogant white bitch.

LOURDES. That's what my mother said.

ROSA. You want to know why your mother left? They were afraid you'd have to go to school with someone like me. There was a saying in Cuba before the revolution. It went, "Go to white." Marry up. Marry someone lighter. So your children can end up white.

LOURDES. And what's the saying now? "Go to black"?

ROSA. No. The revolution changed all that. My color does not matter.

LOURDES. Yes it does. You have to look Mulatta... So you can look exotic to some middle aged German man. So you can sell yourself for twenty dollars.

GLADYS. She does not sell herself. My daughter does not and will never sell herself.

CARLOS. That's why we had a revolution.

LOURDES. Really. They should write a book about her. You must be the only one.

ROSA. I am not the only one.

CARLOS. My daughter is going to be an engineer!

LOURDES. And what will you build anything with?

ROSA. What?

THE COOK

LOURDES. What money? What materials?

ROSA. My pride, and my mind; which are far superior to yours.

LOURDES. Well... Really... Are they?

ROSA. Yes. What do you think about?

LOURDES. Many things.

ROSA. Name some.

LOURDES. That losing this house ruined my mother's chance for happiness. She has been homesick all her life.

GLADYS. She never wrote me a letter. Never once tried to reach me. She handed me seven hundred dollars and expected me to keep this place intact for forty years. And as the years went by, I kept believing in her loyalty. I never even allowed myself to dream of a way to escape any of this. Because I wanted her to have her house when she returned, to have a place that she could recognize and feel safe in. And here it is. I did it.

LOURDES. She's never coming back.

GLADYS. I don't care anymore.

ROSA. If you're not buying lunch, you better go. This is a business. And we've got work to do.

LOURDES. You're kicking me out?

ROSA. Yes. Yes, I am. Get out!

LOURDES. It used to be beautiful. I can tell. Now it's ruined.

(LOURDES is about to take a photo.)

ROSA. Don't you fucking dare.

(LOURDES walks away. ROSA follows her out.)

GLADYS. A cold reality has just left the room.

CARLOS. Finally, you understand the revolution.

(ROSA walks back in.)

GLADYS. She called me a nigger. Rosa? She thought I was a nigger. Not a friend...never even mentioned my name...once she left, she never said Gladys ever again...

ROSA. Let her go. Please, let the past go.

GLADYS. What a fool I've been.

CARLOS. No.

GLADYS. Why not?

CARLOS. You kept it all going.

GLADYS. Have I?

ROSA. All of it. For forty years. For us. We have the most popular paladar in all of La Habana.

GLADYS.Yes, we do.

ROSA. That's right.

CARLOS. I think we should have a better name for it than just our address.

ROSA. I always thought that.

CARLOS. Yes. I agree.

ROSA. We are going to call it "Gladys' Place."

CARLOS. Good.

GLADYS. Why not?

CARLOS. Yes.

ROSA. I'll get an artist to make a sign.

GLADYS. What time is it?

ROSA. Almost noon.

GLADYS.Come on. We've got to get those chickens in the oven.

ROSA. Yes, we do.

GLADYS. Come, Carlos. Time to work.

ROSA. We gotta get the chickens ready.

CARLOS. Yes, we do.

GLADYS. Carlos, keep chopping the onions.

CARLOS. I will.

THE COOK

(They start to prepare the food. ROSA takes out a notebook.)

ROSA.So, how many lemons?
GLADYS. What?
ROSA. For each chicken?
GLADYS. Around two.

(ROSA writes it down.)

GLADYS. Why are you writing it down?
ROSA. 'Cause I want to learn every recipe.
GLADYS. You do? Why?
ROSA. 'Cause I will try to be as good as you are.
CARLOS. Why?
ROSA. 'Cause I'm going to be a cook.
CARLOS. You're going to be an engineer.
ROSA. What good would that do me?
GLADYS. What?
CARLOS. My daughter is going to be a professional.
ROSA. A professional cook. Lourdes is right. What can we build anything with? The future for now is tourism. Even Fidel knows that. And I'd rather be a cook than a whore.
CARLOS. Don't talk like that in front of me.
GLADYS. Two lemons, half an orange, half a lime. Three spoonfuls of oregano and a little cumin, that's my trick, four cloves of garlic and lard placed underneath the skin, salt and pepper...strawberry.
ROSA. What?
GLADYS. It wasn't lime. It was strawberry in 1959.
CARLOS. This is just a special period.
GLADYS. Right.
CARLOS. This is not the end.
GLADYS. Do me a favor, Rosa...
ROSA. Anything...

THE COOK

GLADYS. When you learn everything from me... because I will teach you every trick...

ROSA. Thank you.

GLADYS. Become a cook at a big fancy hotel.

(BLACKOUT.)

END OF PLAY

ADULT ENTERTAINMENT
Elaine May

There is a cloud over porn queen Heidi the Ho's cable TV show. Her guests are mourning the passing of their employer and mentor, a legendary porn film maker. Tired of working for others, this motley group of adult video veterans decides to write and shoot their own extravaganza, an art film. Script one doesn't live up to their expectations so they bring in a new writer, one who insists they read the classics to prepare for their roles. Unexpected light bulbs go off and hilarity escalates. "May's best work ... surprises us with humanity in the midst of the ridiculous.... It's the comedy of the year."—*New York Post*. "Only a frenzied comic mind could imagine ... this delight ... with its giddy, raunchy sense of humor."—*Show Business Weekly*. 3 m., 3 f. (#3835)

MAN IN THE FLYING LAWN CHAIR
Caroline Cromelin, Eric Nightengale, Monica Read, Kimberly Reiss, Troy W. Taber and Toby Wherry

This high-altitude comedy of errors is based on the true story of Larry Walters, a man who secured his place as a cult hero for weird daredevils everywhere by using surplus weather balloons to launch himself to 16,000 feet in an aluminum lawn chair—and lived to tell about it. Developed through improvisation at the 78th Street Theatre Lab, this winner of the Edinburgh Festival's Best of the Fringe was aired on the BBC. 2 m., 3 f. (#14804)

**Send for your copy of the Samuel French
BASIC CATALOGUE OF PLAYS AND MUSICALS**